Do-It-Yourself Tombststones And Markers
with Dale Power

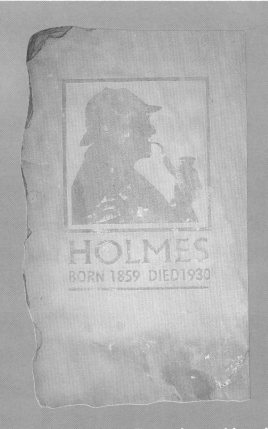

Text written with and photography by Jeffrey B. Snyder

4880 Lower Valley Road, Atglen, PA 19310 USA

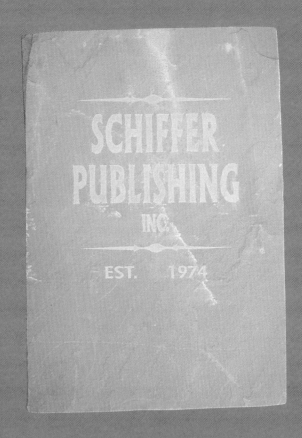

Copyright © 1999 by Dale L. Power
Library of Congress Catalog Card Number:98-88427

Book Designed by Randy L. Hensley
Type set in ZaphChanBdBT/ZaphHumnst BT

ISBN: 0-7643-0745-2
Printed in China

Published by Schiffer Publishing Ltd.
4880 Lower Valley Road
Atglen, PA 19310
Phone: (610) 593-1777; Fax: (610) 593-2002
E-mail: Schifferbk@aol.com
Please visit our web site catalog at www.schifferbooks.com

This book may be purchased from the publisher.
Include $3.95 for shipping.
Please try your bookstore first.
We are interested in hearing from authors
with book ideas on related subjects.
You may write for a free catalog.

In Europe, Schiffer books are distributed by
Bushwood Books
6 Marksbury Rd.
Kew Gardens
Surrey TW9 4JF England
Phone: 44 (0)181 392-8585; Fax: 44 (0)181 392-9876
E-mail: Bushwd@aol.com

Contents

Introduction

Throughout history, people have always looked for ways to mark their passing, to prove they were here, and to memorialize their loved ones' final resting places with monuments of stone or wood. In this book, Dale Power provides you with the tools and techniques to create long lasting, beautiful stone monuments and markers of your own with a sandblaster. While any kind of stone you have on hand may be used, marble, granite, or another other hard stone work best when creating monuments to stand the test of time.

Techniques for cutting both letters and designs into stone are covered in detail. Almost any design that you can carve on wood may be cut in stone. Patterns for design, both old and new, are provided. Your local stone cutter is another good source for patterns ideas ... and for supplies as well. Companies in the business will be listed in your local phone directory under headstones or monuments.

The projects presented in this book are not *all* grave markers. With the sandblaster and a little practice, the options are wide open. For example, you can make markers bearing family names or house numbers and use them in front yards to greet people who come to call. Markers, monuments, and signs, both large and small, of stone or wood, may all be produced following the techniques presented here. Have fun with the markers you make and use!

Tools

Always remember to use safety equipment to protect yourself when working with any equipment that is mentioned in this book or that you may decide to use in making these markers. Tools required to complete these projects include a sandblaster with a medium to narrow nozzle and a sand hopper (either pressure or gravity fed), an air compressor (capable of producing between 40 and 60 pounds of pressure), gauntlet gloves, a face shield, a dust mask, medium standard silicone grit, and large sheets of plastic. Additional tools needed include sandblasting mask, a long straight edge, a pencil, thin cardboard, glue (a glue stick, instant glue and an accelerator), an X-acto knife with an X611 blade, a razor blade, a hammer, wooden or rubber mallet, a screwdriver, safety glasses or goggles, exterior gloss paint, a ketchup dispenser and a paint brush, pine board or pressure treated lumber, a soapstone pencil, and an electric engraver.

Sandblasting Projects

Preparing the Stones, Creating the Masks

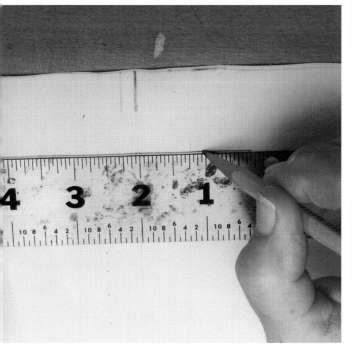

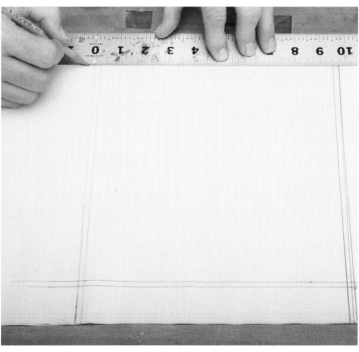

You can lay out a border by hand if you are going to use a graphic of some sort.

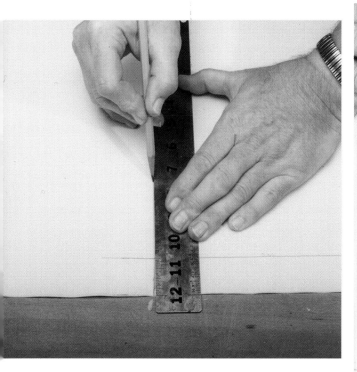

Lay out your design on the sandblasting mask. It is best to use a long straight edge to keep your lines uniform. Since we are going to cut this design out on the stone, you can overrun your lines when drawing.

If you wish to use an illustration, you may use a photocopier to enlarge that image to the proper size.

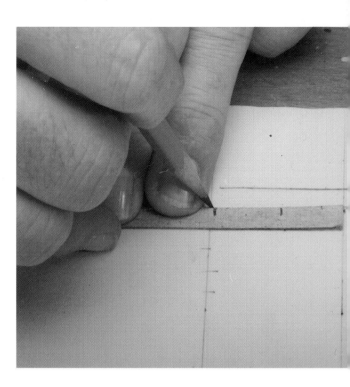

There are several different methods you can use to transfer letters onto your mask. One method involves cutting a piece of thin cardboard to the width of the uprights of the letters. Use your cardboard guide to establish the width of the first upright.

To transfer the illustration to the mask, first lay the illustration over the mask. Then employ the dot to dot method to transfer the design. This method works very well by perforating the edge of your illustration with the tip of your pencil, transferring the image's outline to the underlying mask.

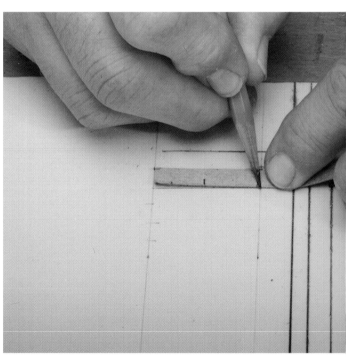

Mark the height of your letter on your cardboard guide. This will assure that all of your letters are the same height. By turning the guide at a right angle, you can establish the letter's width as well.

Connect all of the dots with a pencil line.

Establish the total width of the letter. In this case the letter's width is exactly the same as the height.

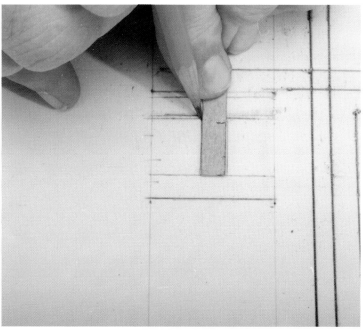

Establish the center of your letter. In this case, the letter is an H. Draw in the letter's center.

Establish the second upright and the center of the letter.

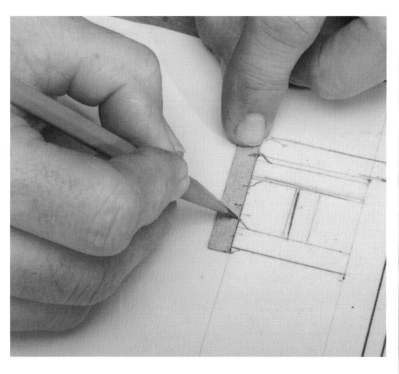

Establish how far out the serifs will extend and mark these locations on your guide.

Draw in the serifs (extensions found on certain letter typefaces which give them a more ornate appearance).

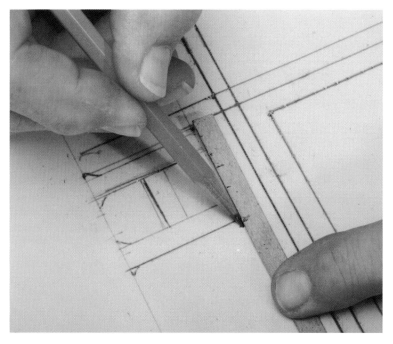

Flip the guide over to the top of the letter and establish the width of the serifs.

If you have a photocopier and the font available, you can place the letters over the mask and use the dot to dot method to transfer them. This may speed up the process for you.

Complete the dot to dot transfer for all of the words on a given line at the same time. if there are multiple lines, work your way down one line at a time. Connecting the dots on the mask.

Finish connecting all of the dots.

All of the letters from the first line are now in place.

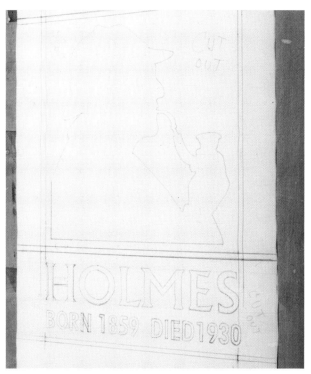

The image is laid out on the mask. The mask is ready to be placed on the stone.

Another way to transfer letters to the mask is even more direct. Lettering may be secured to the mask with a glue stick, making sure that you apply glue to the back of the letters and not to the mask.

Gently press the paper to the mask.

For working ease, remove all excess paper that is not adhered.

The excess paper is removed and the mask is ready to be applied to the stone.

Lay the mask over the stone and, feeling through the mask, properly align the lettering and graphic on the stone (making sure it will all fit).

Remove the paper backing from the mask to expose the adhesive backing prior to applying the mask to the stone.

When cutting your mask, always cut away from inside corners to avoid cutting into the letter.

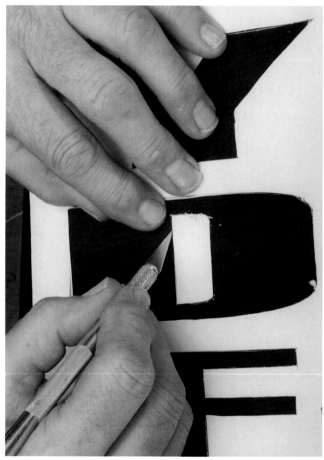

Use an X-acto knife with an X611 blade when cutting tight areas on your mask.

Long straight areas can be cut with a razor blade.

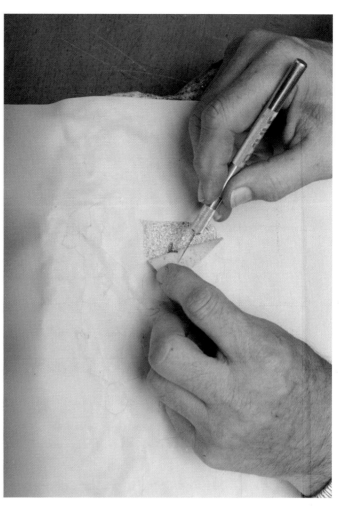

Begin removing the letters from the mask. This stone will be sandblasted into a negative relief. The letters will be cut down into the stone. The areas remaining covered by the mask will not be cut.

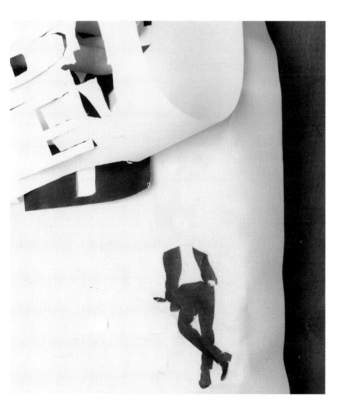

Now for the moment of truth! Lift the paper pattern away to see how well you cut the mask.

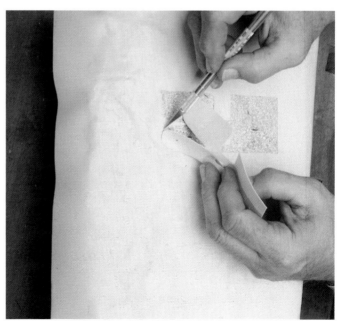

Lift the letters gently, making sure they are cut free all around.

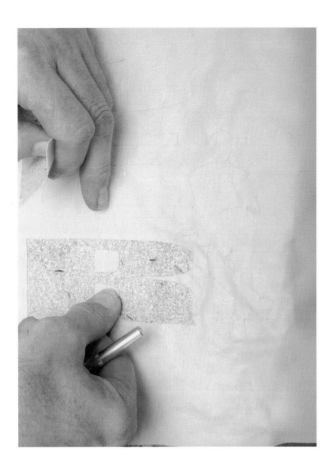

Press around the outside edges of the letters, making sure the remaining mask is adhered to the stone.

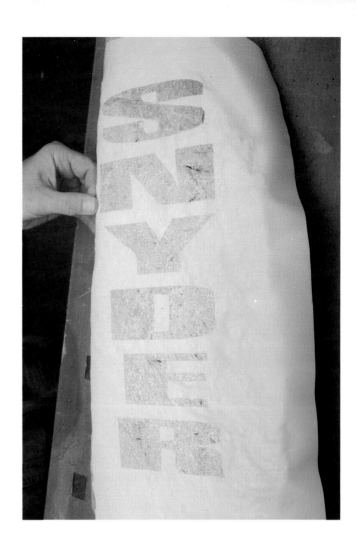

Once the mask is removed, you start to get a feel for the end product's appearance.

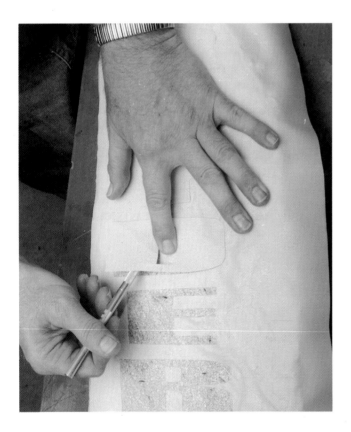

For letters such as A, B, D, O, P, Q, and R, make sure to hold the center of the letter in place while removing the rest from around it.

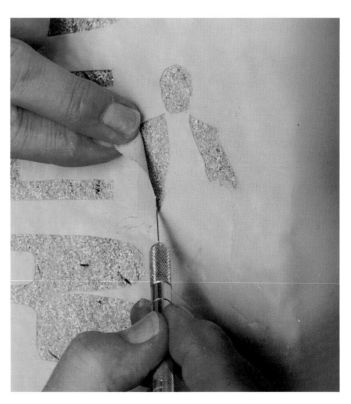

Extra care must be taken when removing graphics. Their many different angles make them more challenging to remove.

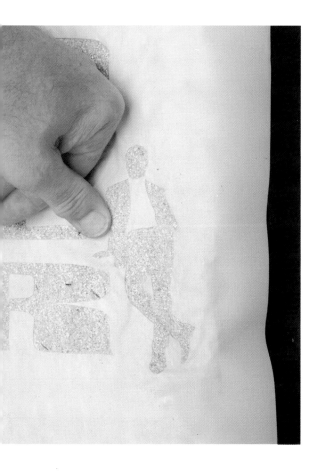

One final check to make sure the mask is firmly in place.

Cover any areas of the stone left exposed with scrap mask prior to sandblasting.

This stone is almost ready for the sandblaster.

Before we blast, a few words about additional stone preparations. If you are lucky, you will find a fairly smooth stone...like our last one. Otherwise, as is the case with this sedimentary stone, some preparation work will be required prior to sandblasting.

Tools needed to prepare this stone include a hammer, a wooden or rubber mallet, a screwdriver, and a tool with a finer tip. Also, whenever you are working with stone like this, make sure to wear safety glasses or goggles.

Tap gently with your mallet, carefully removing excess stone.

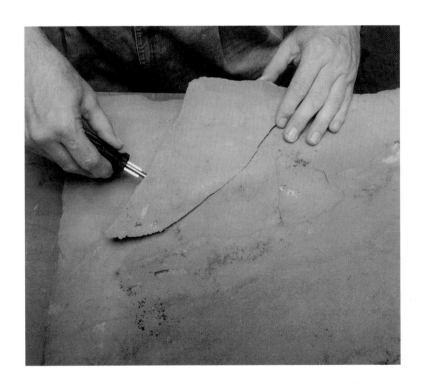

Sedimentary stones (including sandstone, slate, and mudstone) are fairly easy to smooth as the layers lift off in sheets. Begin smoothing the stone, lifting away unwanted layers.

Watch closely, fossils (including small shells like this) sometime show up in these sedimentary layers.

You find an area of the stone that will not come loose easily, [ge]ntly tap it with a hammer to loosen it.

To ensure that the mask will adhere to the stone, it is best to wash the newly smoothed rock face to remove any excess dust or dirt.

The stone is clean and drying.

[Aft]er you achieve a smooth surface, go back and check for small [bum]ps.

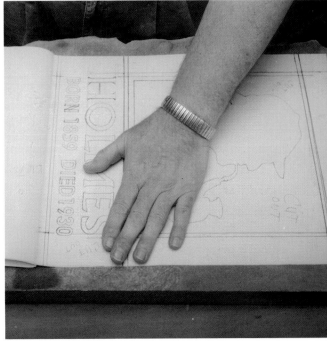

Partially strip the mask off the backing and ...

Progressing on, removing the remaining backing from the mask. The mask falls into place this way as the backing is removed.

lay it down, making sure that it is solidly adhered to the stone.

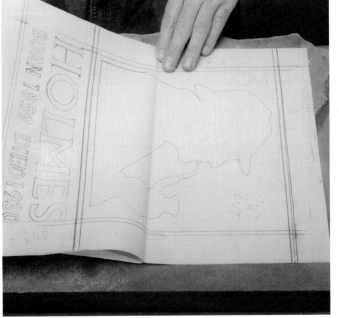

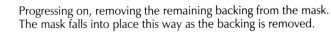

Cut out carefully around the letters.

Start to expose the background, leaving the areas covered that are to be protected by the masking.

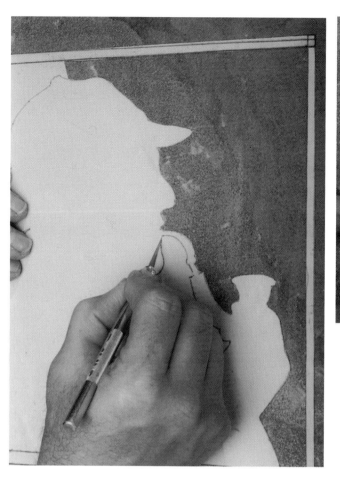

Work carefully around these small letters. Remove the centers of the letters first.

Remove the mask from around the graphic in sections, making sure the wrong pieces are not lifted away.

The graphic is cut out. This is going to be a positive (or raised) image. The background is going to be reduced during sandblasting.

Off to the sandblaster this piece goes! As a rule of thumb, when reducing the background you cannot blast any deeper than twice the width of your thinnest line.

I am working on a third project as well. As a suggestion, when cutting curved letters, use a finer blade such as this X-acto blade.

If you make the mistake of removing and throwing away the wrong part of the letter ...

Some of the smaller letters are in place. The sharper, finer blade made this possible.

a correction can be made by cutting a new piece of mask to replace the mistakenly removed portion. If you happen to have second copy of the letter it is easier to cut that new replacemen piece.

Here is a friendly word of advice. Look your mask over very carefully for stray cuts. If you find any, they can be patched by placing a strip of the mask over them.

Patching the mistake.

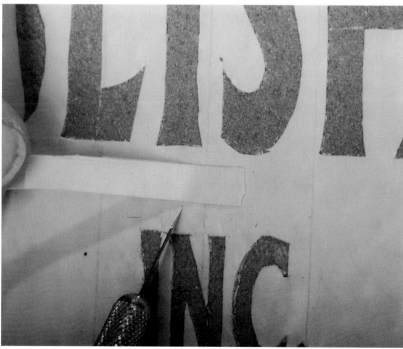

Like so.

See? Now you can't even tell there was a mistake!

You can add to your layout at any time. Establish a line to level the additional lettering and carefully applying the new text along that line.

Our third stone is ready for sandblasting.

Adding the new letters. Make sure your blade is sharp.

Sandblasting the Stones & Finishing Touches

Now that we are ready to start sandblasting, a few of the items you will need include a sandblaster with a sand hopper attached to it (this hopper can be either pressure or gravity fed), an air compressor that will produce between 40 and 60 pounds of pressure, gloves to protect your hands and arms, a face shield to protect your face from bouncing grit, and a dust mask to protect your lungs. The medium standard silicone grit is a good all around abrasive. The large sheets of plastic shown here make it easy to retrieve the grit for later reuse.

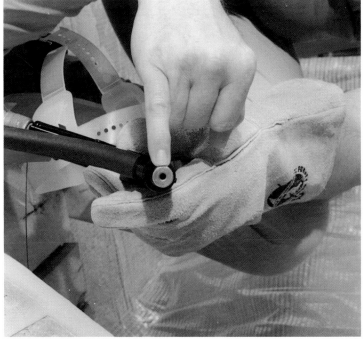

Use a medium to small size nozzle for this work.

Hold your nozzle 4 to 6 inches from the stone, depending on the weight of the line that has been cut (stay back 6" for light lines and close in to 4" for heavy cutting). Hold your nozzle at a 90 degree angle to the surface to avoid undercutting.

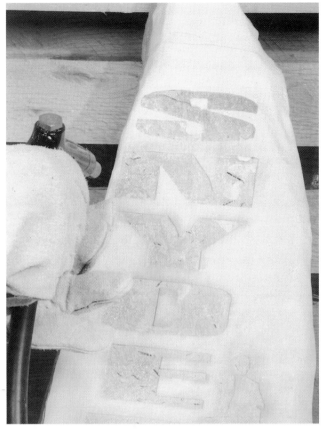

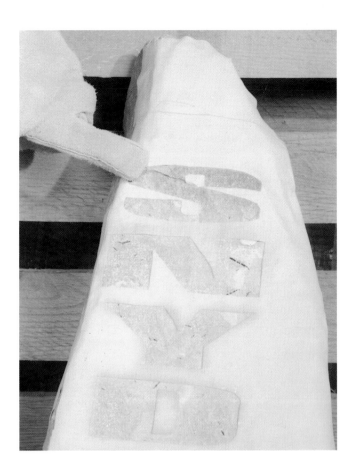

Even if your stone has an uneven area exposed, you can reduce that down to make a smooth surface.

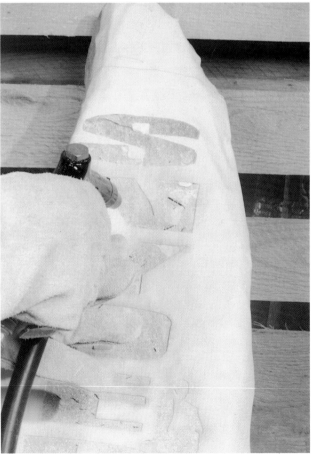

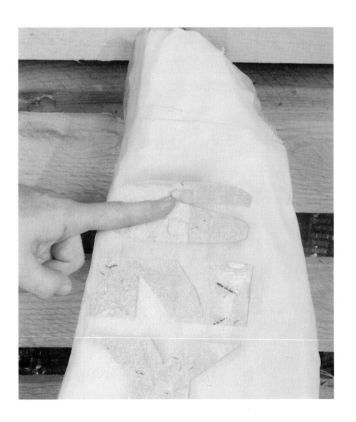

A word of advice: keep the nozzle moving to avoid cutting too deeply.

The raised area has been reduced.

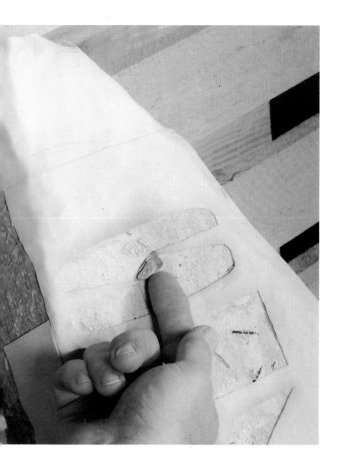

If the worst case scenario occurs and some of your stone flakes away, you can repair it ...

and an accelerator.

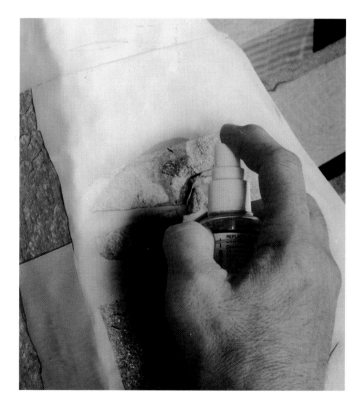

with an instant glue...

Lightly spray the accelerator on one side, holding the spray nozzle 8" to 10" from the area.

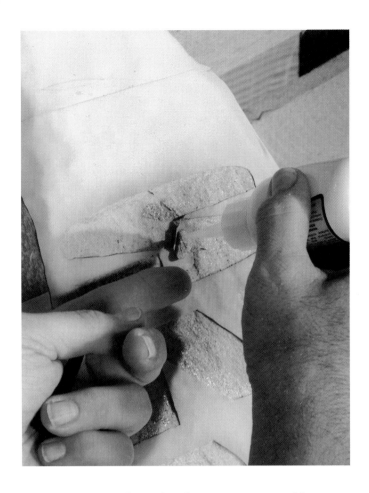

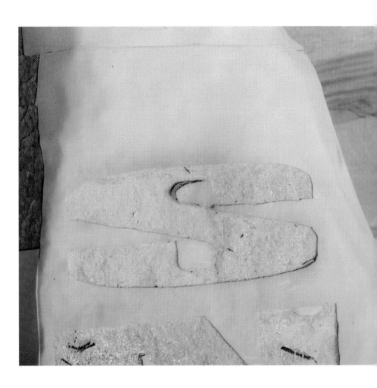

The piece is glued back into place and work may continue.

Apply your instant glue to the other area. Be very careful not to get the glue on your hands and touch the accelerator because bonding is instantaneous.

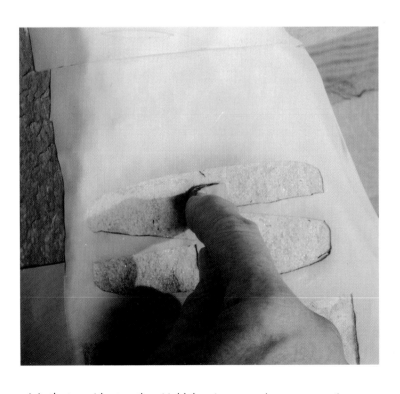

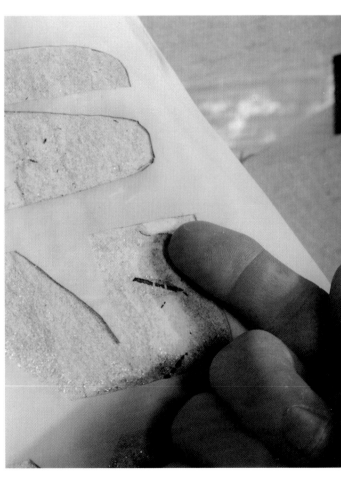

Join the two sides together. Hold the pieces together momentarily.

Examine your work carefully, looking for areas that still need to be reduced.

This area has been successfully reduced. Remember to keep the nozzle moving back and forth over to avoid digging too deep in any one spot.

If you wish, the letters may now be filled with paint to make them stand out more against the background of the stone.

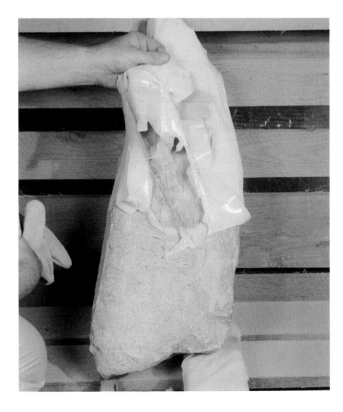

The stone has been successfully sandblasted. Carefully remove *all* of the masking.

I am adding an exterior gloss black paint to the areas that have been sandblasted away will make the letters stand out. First make sure the stone is level.

If the paint does not spread smoothly, you can help it along with paint brush.

A ketchup dispenser is a wonderful tool for this job, delivering paint into all the appropriate sandblasted areas.

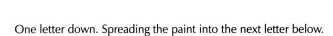

Make sure you start where your hands won't drag through the paint, either working from the top down or from left to right as needed (left to right that is *if* you are right handed).

One letter down. Spreading the paint into the next letter below.

Be careful when working in shallow spots. The paint brush will help keep the paint within the boundaries of the letters.

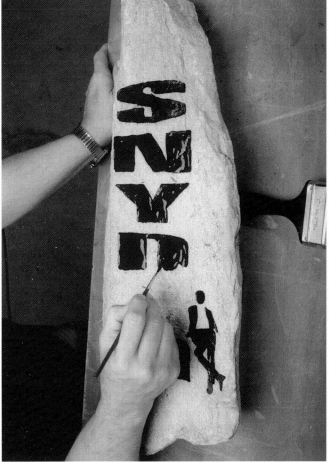

Work your way down the stone.

Once you have finished the letters, you may need to clean up in areas where paint has overrun the edges.

After the paint has dried, gently remove the unwanted paint from the stone with a sharp tool.

As you can see, the paint has overrun the edges of the R in one place.

The letter is cleaned, the unwanted paint has been removed.

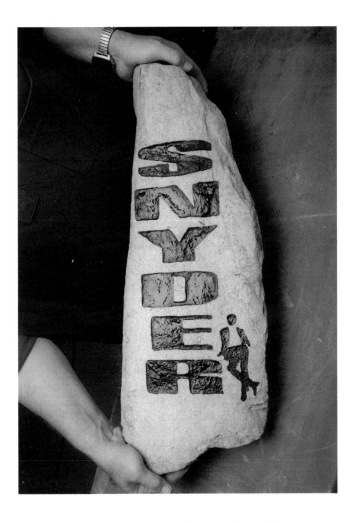

The painted lettering on the stone is complete.

For the "Holmes" project we are going to reduce the background, making this a positive instead of a negative image. Everything covered in the white mask will be raised, all exposed surfaces will be dropped back.

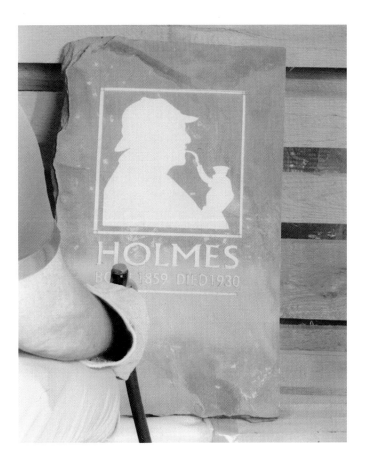

Begin to reduce away the exposed stone with the sandblaster as before.

Slowly work your way up the stone, controlling the depth of your cut.

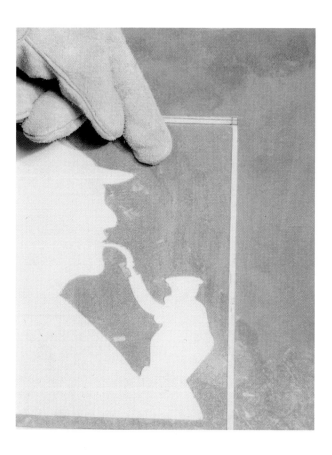

Keep a close watch when you see a discoloration in the stone to make sure that both areas of the stone are of the same hardness. If they are not, one area will cut faster than the other. If the stone is softer in one area, you must move the nozzle more quickly over the area of softer stone to avoid cutting too deeply.

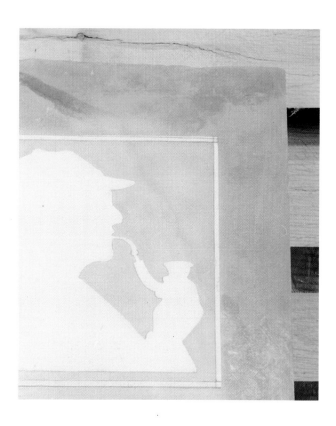

As you can see, both areas have now been reduced.

This area illustrates the difference in the hardness of stone that can occur. The brownish area is a harder stone and requires more attention to bring it down.

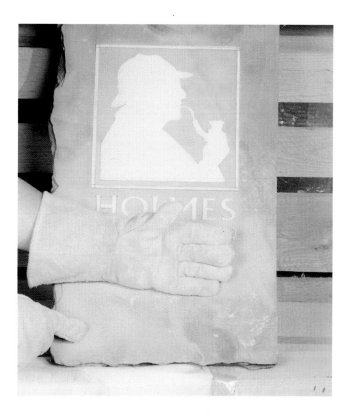

Don't worry about reducing the base of the stone as this will be set into the ground and will not show.

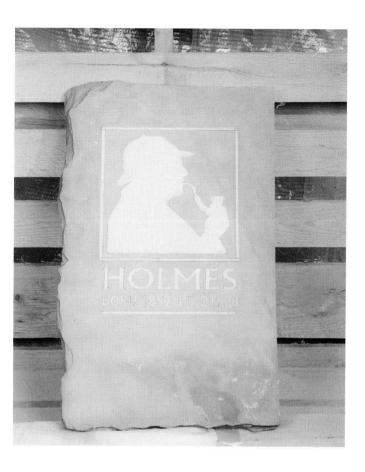

Now we have finished reducing the stone and are ready to strip off the masking. You won't be absolutely sure how effective your efforts have been until the mask comes off.

The stone is completed. Now we can clean up the white chisel marks with a little water and a brush.

Remove the mask to reveal your handy work.

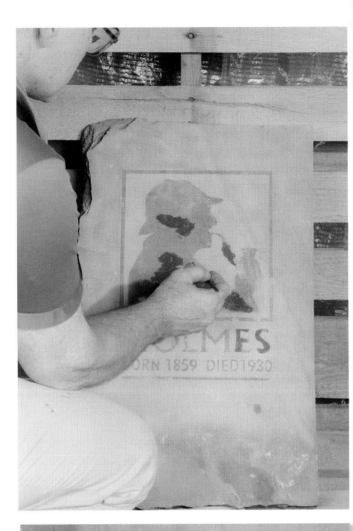

You can clean the individual letters with a small brush to remove any dust that has collected on them. Don't worry about water spreading out onto the surrounding stone. When it dries, the entire stone will return to its dry color.

Cleaning the larger areas of the graphic that were marred when the stone was smoothed.

This publishing house project is a fairly straight-forward sandblasting job. There are very few fine lines; therefore, you should be able to get a very uniform surface on your cuts.

Working my way down the stone.

...am starting at the top and working down. As before, try to ...aintain a uniform cut depth by keeping the sandblaster's nozzle ...n motion at all times. One way to tell if your cut is uniform is to ...ook for the discoloration on the mask. If it is discolored all ...round, you have cut the entire piece.

Note the difference in the coloration between the sandblasted letters (which are lighter) and the letters yet to be cut.

I have finished sandblasting and the stone is ready for stripping. Peeling away the mask.

The Holmes stone is complete as well.

The completed stone.

Along one edge, adhere the graphic to the board with masking tape.

We will layout another pattern to be sandblasted on this pine board. If you are making a marker for outdoor use, you should use pressure treated lumber. Begin the project by roughly cutting the mask to fit the size of the board.

Transfer the graphic to the mask with carbon paper for a change of pace.

Apply the mask to the board prior to placing any graphics on it.

Use a pencil to trace the graphic.

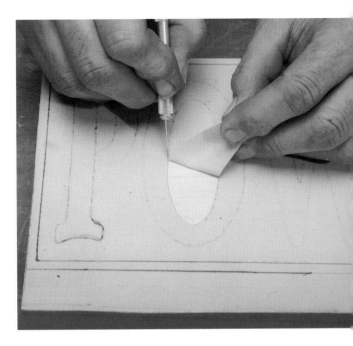

Cut and remove the mask from the areas you wish to reduce with the sandblaster. You should know that the mask sticks tightly to the wood.

The pattern is transferred.

This board is ready to go to the sandblaster. This piece could be a monument for a pet or even a sign over your door.

Note how the sandblaster is beginning to eat away the wood around the base of the letters. Continue to reduce the background wood away around the letters.

hen you start to sandblast wood, extreme care should be taken
 make sure that your sandblaster is at exactly 90 degrees to the
ood and that you do not try to remove too much wood at any
 e time. You may even wish to use a separate piece of wood to
 st and perfect your blasting technique before beginning on your
 t piece. Adjust your compressor, 40 to 60 pounds of pressure is
 ough. Too much pressure from the compressor will undercut
 e wood too quickly.

Depending on the wood that you are using, the sand may remove the softer wood between the growth rings faster. If your wood has a lot of grain, the end result will add considerable interest to your piece.

The sandblasting is finished. Leave the mask in place until the plaque has been painted.

The background on the wooden plaque may be spray painted or hand painted. Just leave the mask in place until the job is done to ensure that the letters and graphics remain clean.

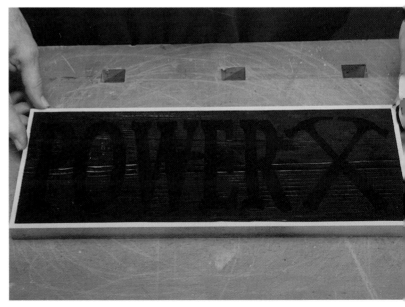

Pull back the mask, exposing the unpainted wood.

Remove the mask carefully.

The wooden sign is done.

Engraving on Stone

A soapstone pencil and an electric engraver may also be used to apply a design on a rock. Soapstone pencils are available at almost any welding supply store.

When using the electric engraver to place the design into the stone, remember to wear safety goggles to protect your eyes fr[om] flying stone chips.

The image is drawn onto the stone using the soapstone pencil. You can be adventurous with this design. If part of the image is not to your liking, it may be easily wiped away and redrawn.

Most electric engravers come with a control to adjust the dept[h] the engraving. You may have to experiment with the control t[o] your best depth. Follow your outline and have fun making y[our] piece stand out from the surrounding stone. You can add shadowing and other details to make your image appear mor[e] three dimensional.

The amount of shading you apply is a matter of personal taste. Apply enough to make the central pattern stand out. Think of this as drawing with chalk on rock. You need enough "color" to make the image stand out from the surrounding rock.

Engraving the shadows of the eye sockets.

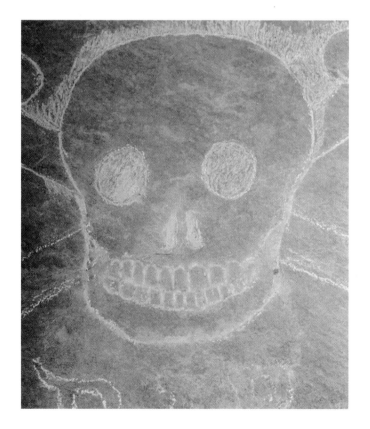

Note the shadowing. See how the leg bone stands out from the surrounding engraved surface. By engraving in different directions, you can create different patterns that will suggest greater or lesser shadowing.

The grinning skull is engraved.

Engraving the lower leg around the knee joint. Adding shadow to enhance the image.

Refresh your marks as needed. Most of my R.I.P. had been rubbed away while engraving the skull and cross bones.

A paint brush is ideal for sweeping away the stone dust created during engraving. Keep this dust cleared away so that you can clearly see the results of your engraving as the work progresses.

Engraving the lettering.

A small paint brush and a little water will remove excess stone dust, making your image more distinct.

The finished skull and cross bones motif stone, ready to be installed in its outside home.

As the water dries, the engraved lines (which turn dark when wet) regain their distinctive light shade.

Gallery

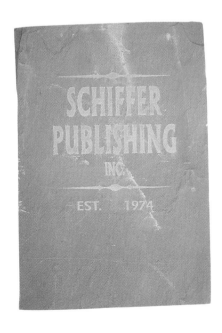

Cemeteries are full of distinctive designs sure to inspire every sandblaster.

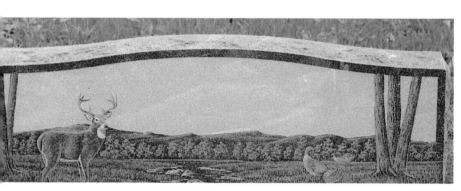

48

BLEST BE
THE TIE
THAT BINDS

53

ABCDEFGHIJKLMNO PQRSTUVWXYZabcd efghijklmnopqrstuv wxyz

ABCDEFGHIJKLM NOPQRSTUVWXY Zabcdefghijklmno pqrstuvwxyz

1234567 8910

1234567 8901

1234567 8910

123456789

10123456

78910

12345678910

123456789

1012345678

910

ABCDEFGHIJ
KLMNOPQRS
cdefghijklmn
opqrstuvwxyz
ABCDEFGHIJKLM
NOPQRSTUVWXY
Zabcdefghijklmn
opqrstuvwxyz
ABCDEFGHIJ

KLMNOPQRS
TUVWXYZ

ABCDEFGHIJ
KLMNOPQRS
TUVWXYZ

ABCDEFGHIJK
LMNOPQRSTU
VWXYZabcdefg
hijklmnopqrstu

VWXYZ
ABCDEFGHIJKL
MNOPQRSTUV
WXYZabcdefghi
jklmnopqrstuvw
xyz

ABCDEFGHIJK
LMNOPQRSTU

VWXYZabcdefg

hijklmnopqrstuv

wxyz

ABCDEFGHIJ

KLMNOPQRS

TUVWXYZabc

defghijklmno

pqrstuvwxyz